3

Seamus Heaney

Warren Hope

GREENWICH EXCHANGE

Greenwich Exchange, London

First published in Great Britain in 2002
Reprinted 2004
All rights reserved

Seamus Heaney
© Warren Hope 2002

Printed and bound by Q3 Digital/Litho, Loughborough
Tel: 01509 213456
Typesetting and layout by Albion Associates, London
Tel: 020 8852 4646
Cover design by December Publications, Belfast
Tel: 028 90286559

Cover: Photograph of Seamus Heaney © www.bigglasseye.co.uk

Greenwich Exchange Website: www.greenex.co.uk

ISBN 1-871551-37-4

In memory of Bronson Feldman,
teacher and friend

CONTENTS

Chronology

1939   Born on 13th April at Mossbawn, the family farm in County Derry, Northern Ireland.

1945-51   Attends Anahorish Primary School.

1951-57   Attends St Columb's College on scholarship as a boarder.

1957-61   Attends Queen's University, Belfast, and takes a First in English.

1961   Qualifies as a teacher and begins a teaching career.

1963-66   Teaches at St Joseph's College and joins the so-called Belfast Group of poets led by Philip Hobsbaum.

1965   Marries Marie Devlin.

1966   *Death of a Naturalist* published and first child born.

1969   *Door into the Dark* published; Heaney goes to Europe on a Somerset Maugham Award.

1970-71   Visiting professor at the University of California, Berkeley.

1972   Moves to County Wicklow in the Republic of Ireland; *Wintering Out* published.

1975   *North* published. Teaches at the Carysfort Teacher Training College in Dublin where he becomes a department head.

1976   Moves to Dublin.

1979   *Field Work* published; visiting professor at Harvard University.

1980   *Poems 1965-1975* and the collection of prose, *Preoccupations*, published.

1981   Resigns from Carysfort College and joins Field Day, the theatre company founded by Brian Friel and Stephen Rea.

1982   Begins teaching at Harvard University.

1983   *Sweeney Astray* published.

1984   Appointed Boylston Professor of Rhetoric and Oratory at Harvard; *Station Island* published; Margaret Heaney, the poet's mother, dies.

1986   Patrick Heaney, the poet's father, dies.

1987   *The Haw Lantern* published.

1988   *Government of the Tongue*, a collection of prose, published.

1989-94 Delivers lectures as Professor of Poetry at Oxford University.

1990   *Selected Poems 1966-1987* published; *The Cure at Troy* performed by Field Day Theatre Company.

1991   *Seeing Things* published.

1995   Awarded the Nobel Prize for Literature.

1996   *The Spirit Level* published; resigns the professorship at Harvard and is appointed Emerson Poet in Residence there.

1998   *Opened Ground: Poems 1966-1996* published.

1999   *Beowulf* published.

2001   *Electric Light* published.

1

Death of a Naturalist

Seamus Heaney's long-time friend, Seamus Deane, wrote in *The New Yorker* that as an undergraduate Heaney was "always 'well-in' with those in power – teachers, professors, and the like." Nonetheless, Deane recalled, in private Heaney was rebellious, making fun of and laughing at those in power. Deane attributes Heaney's youthful ambivalence toward the powerful to a fundamental contradiction in Heaney's character. This ambivalence is said to be the result of "Heaney's way of dealing with his own contradictory sense of himself: his authority and his uncertainty."

This contradiction seems to be at the root of Seamus Heaney's career to date. The career is a success story, after all, and, as a result, a certain glamour emanates from it. It is not a rags-to-riches story, exactly, but rather an obscurity-to-celebrity story. It is likely that Heaney's uncertainty has driven him to seek public recognition. This uncertainty accounts for his frequent interviews (Ian Hamilton accurately describes him as "the most over-interviewed of living poets"), the lectures, the academic posts and honours, the reliance on what Heaney has called "craft and determination" in the production of verses, the ambition to erect relatively large poetic structures, and so on. Heaney's authority, on the other hand, turns up in individual, primarily private, poems or even in single lines. In short, this contradiction does much to explain the disparity between Heaney's public reputation and his achievement.

His combination of uncertainty and authority shows up early.

1

It is present in Heaney's first, and at least arguably still his best, full-length book of poems, *Death of a Naturalist*, published in 1966.

I

Seamus Heaney was born on 13th April 1939, about thirty miles from Belfast, in County Derry, Northern Ireland. He is the eldest of nine children born to Patrick and Margaret Kathleen Heaney. They lived on the family farm of about fifty acres called 'Mossbawn', where Heaney had been born.

The part Heaney's childhood plays in his poetry can hardly be overestimated. His mother and father are present not only as characters in some of the poems but are also the inspiration for many of them. As the eldest child and a son, he no doubt carried with him much of the hopes and ambitions of his parents throughout his life. He has spoken of his childhood as a "den" life, enclosed, tight-knit, and cut off but happy, if not Edenic. The language and reticence of his childhood influenced his poetry by providing not only themes but also a linguistic distinctiveness.

Heaney's earliest years were the years of the Second World War. Many of the images of warfare and violence in his early poems no doubt arise from boyhood memories and imaginings. The role of the radio in his early den life also meant much to him. Alien voices coming through the airwaves brought a sense of the magic of language as well as news of the war into the home.

Being raised as a Roman Catholic in Northern Ireland also shaped Heaney's imagination and determined the slant of his education. Although often described as an agnostic poet, the imagery of the church is part of Heaney's imagery from the beginning. And although Heaney has described poetry as a kind of "grace", his training could have convinced him of the possibility of poetic salvation through 'works' as well, helping to account for the sheer amount of his verse and his need to write even when he has little or nothing to say.

Heaney's formal education began when he attended the Anahorish School, in 1945, the last year of the war. Heaney later commemorated the place-name of the school in a poem. Catholics and Protestants both attended the school and Heaney began the study of Latin there. He remembered his Latin teacher, Master Bernard Murphy, when he wrote 'Station Island'.

If Heaney had been born in a slightly earlier period, his education might well have stopped there. Perhaps he would have worked the farm and dealt in cattle, following in his father's footsteps. Perhaps he would have gone on to become a priest, the hope for the eldest son in many Irish Catholic families. These possible alternative careers provide the basis for 'Digging', one of Heaney's best-known poems which originally appeared as the first poem in his first book.

The Northern Ireland Education Act of 1947, however, made it possible for Heaney to continue his education. Attending on a scholarship, Heaney became a boarder at St Columb's College in Londonderry, or Derry, one of the placenames in Northern Ireland that reflects the conflicts there.

Seamus Deane first met Heaney at St Columb's in 1950 and describes the school this way:

> St Columb's College is a diocesan grammar school for [Catholic] boys in the city of Derry (as we called it), or Londonderry (as the official title had it). Derry is only a few miles from the border that separates Northern Ireland from the Republic of Ireland. It has a historical resonance for Protestants, because they endured a famous siege there in 1689 by the Catholic armies of King James II, and also for Catholics, because between 1922 and 1972 the city was notorious for discriminating against the local Catholic majority.

It was neither political conflicts nor historical associations that were dominant when Heaney attended the school, however. More important for his poetry and for an understanding of it is his memory that he was homesick for two years when he first attended St Columb's. The shock that accompanied his removal from the den undoubtedly contributed to his sense of uncertainty. He was a boarder because his home was so far away from the school and it seems clear that 'country hick' was one of the earliest roles he felt obliged to play in public, just as the day boys played the part of 'city slickers'.

When asked by Karl Miller during an interview whether his boarding-school experience was repressive, Heaney replied:

> Oh it was, yes. We didn't know it was. We were like chaps in a barracks. Boarders as we were, many of us from small farms, born into quite religious homes, growing up in an environment where the priest was a respected figure and the mysteries of the faith still retained a power to silence you. We were pre-formed, you might say, to fit the regime. Morning mass, bells to summon you to class, night prayers, silence in the study hall, the struggle with 'bad thoughts'.

Nonetheless, the school provided him with a strong multi-lingual literary education and prepared him to pass the examinations that permitted him to win a bursary to attend Queen's University in Belfast. In fact, Heaney delayed attending Queen's to spend an additional year at St Columb's. It was during this additional year that, according to Seamus Deane, Heaney had the good fortune to study with Sean B. O'Kelly,

> a man of such sweetness and enthusiasm that even at sixteen or seventeen years of age we appreciated how fortunate we were to have him. He took us through Chaucer's *General Prologue to the Canterbury Tales*, *Hamlet*, *Paradise Lost*, Wordsworth and Keats, Lamb and Hazlitt, Hardy, Hopkins, Tennyson, and Arnold. Since our scholarships had already been won, all we needed to aim for was a State Exhibition, which provided an additional financial boon. It was a perfect year.

If there is no evidence that Heaney began to write at St Columb's, it is clear that he began to understand the relationship between literature and life there. He first wrote, or at least published, poems when he was an undergraduate at Queen's University, Belfast.

II

When Philip Larkin was asked why he had chosen poetry, he replied, "I didn't choose poetry. Poetry chose me." 'Digging' suggests that Seamus Heaney chose poetry and in a slightly ambivalent way, tainted with a sense of guilt. The poem is the first one in *Death of a Naturalist* and is a poem of dedication to a career if not a calling. The poem opens in a rather startling way, with the poet self-dramatising himself as a country man if not a hard-boiled tough guy.

The opening pictures the poet as a slightly wild, exotic creature, a boarder among day boys:

> Between my finger and my thumb
> The squat pen rests; snug as a gun.

This combination of a plain statement of fact and a startling simile is equivalent to Heaney's combination of authority and uncertainty. The statement of fact carries authority. The simile is slightly over the top, an uncertain young man's overreaction to the fear of appearing 'literary' in public. The combination was originally startling, arresting, and acceptable in the work of a young poet. But in retrospect the simile is also a red flag, a warning of difficulties that would dog Heaney's career.

The simile of the gun disappears from the poem, never to return. It has such force, however, such memorability, that its absence at the poem's conclusion serves as the point of the poem.

The poet's dedication is accompanied by a transformation, from the potential use of the pen for violent purposes to its use for cultivation. Both are metaphors for writing, for poetry, but the transformation is worked by the bulk of the poem, and that is the story or memory of a very different, non-literary, back-breaking way of life, the way of the spade, literal cultivation of the earth.

What diverts the poem along this transforming course is a sound heard by the poet, "a clean rasping sound/When the spade sinks into gravelly ground:/My father, digging." The sound heard in the present conjures a memory of the poet's father digging, rather than the actuality of it. It is the poet's skill that gives the memory a concrete, ever-present existence:

> The coarse boot nestled on the lug, the shaft
> Against the inside knee was levered firmly.

This description, based mostly on the accurate use of nouns and verbs, is a lively and living description that culminates in the union of father and son, of digger and poet, or perhaps of the poet as a boy with his brothers and sisters united by communal labour:

> He rooted out tall tops, buried the bright edge deep
> To scatter new potatoes that we picked,
> Loving their cool hardness in our hands.

This act of memory carries the poet back to his early "den life", from the singular of the present ("my finger and my thumb") to the plural of the past ("Loving their cool hardness in our hands"). The pen has been metaphorically put down to take up the potato, not the gun. But the act of memory is also a metaphor for digging, not only the work of the father but also the title of the poem. Digging for potatoes, it is suggested, is analogous to rooting in one's past for words. This first act of memory takes the poet further back – or deeper – to a memory of his father's father. This deeper memory is again introduced by two lines, but lines that are colloquial rather than literary and that use a simile to affirm the identity of forebears rather than the similarity of different implements:

> By God, the old man could handle a spade.
> Just like his old man.

The memory of the poet's grandfather cutting turf in a bog culminates in a description of the poet's current state, a metaphorical combining of the way of life of his ancestors with his own present mental outlook, an outlook described as something of a dilemma:

> The cold smell of potato mould, the squelch and slap
> Of soggy peat, the curt cuts of an edge
> Through living roots awaken in my head.
> But I've no spade to follow men like them.

Is it literally true that it was the want of a spade that kept Seamus Heaney from following the way of life of his father, his grandfather, and men like them? Of course not. If he wished to he could have put down the pen and taken up the spade. It was the presence of the pen in his hand, his education, that separated him from the way of life of his father and grandfather and that introduced a sense of guilt, of betrayal, as well as pride. The ending of the poem represents a compromise, a dedication to follow men like them metaphorically, by digging with the pen. The implication is that the poet will find his living material among the severed roots that have been awakened in his head, the roots of family life and the roots of words. Heaney's uncertainty and authority as a poet spring from these severed roots.

One of Heaney's most ardent critical supporters, Helen Vendler, says of this poem:

> The disturbing thing about 'Digging' is that the Irish Catholic child grew up between the offers of two instruments: the spade and the gun. "Choose," said two opposing voices from his culture: "Inherit the farm," said agricultural tradition; "Take up arms," said Republican militarism.

Vendler goes on to congratulate Heaney on his choice: "It is significant that ... Heaney rejects the concept of writing as aggression, and chooses the spade as the final analogue for his pen ... "

This interpretation is too brightly coloured by events in Northern Ireland that took place after the poem was written and published. It seems to me more likely that the simile of the gun is, as I've suggested, the anti-literary bravado of a bookish young man. If a more concrete source for the simile is desired, the memory of the feel of the gun in the hands of the poet as a boy on or near the family farm is a more likely candidate than the direct action of revolutionary politics. Assassinations and terrorist acts do not seem to me at all present in this poem by a man who took a First in English at Queen's University and earned his living as a teacher. Quite the contrary, what Heaney lingers on and loves is a way of life that is dying if not dead, never to be resurrected: agrarian, provincial, and a source of nostalgia if not of homesickness. More importantly, the dilemma the poem faces and tries to metaphorically resolve is the result of a choice offered the boy by the culture that Vendler dismisses – the choice provided by educational opportunity.

III

Heaney emerged as a poet while an undergraduate at Queen's University, Belfast. He attended the University from 1957 (two years after Philip Larkin left the library there to take up his post at Hull and publish *The Less Deceived*) – until 1961, five years before Heaney published his first book. He first published poems in a literary magazine at Queen's in 1959. Seamus Deane remembered the start of it this way:

> As undergraduates, we began to write poems and, especially in the long summer vacation, to exchange them. Then, in our second year, we started publishing our work in student magazines. At this stage, almost all Heaney's poems were pastiches, poems molded on the contours of poems of writers he favored, Hopkins, Frost, and Dylan Thomas being the ones I recall most from then.

These influences Deane identifies remain present in some of the poems – and some of the best poems – in *Death of a Naturalist*, although it would be well to add Wordsworth to the list. (Deane records that he and Heaney had *Tintern Abbey* by heart at St Columb's.) A playful use of language and a starting point outside the mainstream characterize all of these influences. On the other hand, by the time Heaney came to them they were all popular and respected figures. Heaney no doubt felt a kinship with both their beginnings as outsiders and with their ultimate academic acceptance. Although he read poetry, and especially contemporary poetry, widely at Queen's, there is no sign that he became an enthusiast for unknown or forgotten figures. He found his models from the curriculum.

This tendency is of a piece with his outstanding academic record. He seems to have been a serious, sober, and industrious undergraduate. Achieving First Class Honours in English is one sign of his industry. His being awarded the McMullen Medal for academic achievement is another. Deane's memories again put flesh on the person who performed these accomplishments:

> … Heaney did not drink, became an official of the university Catholic Students' Society, attended lectures, went to the library, wrote his essays.

If Heaney's uncertainty propelled him to be something of a grind as an undergraduate, there were people around who were quick to recognize the gleam of authority in his early verses. He seems to have again been fortunate in at least one of his teachers, Laurence Lerner, a South African and a poet and critic. Lerner seems to have early recognized Heaney's ability and seriousness and neatly expressed his view to Seamus Deane by saying Heaney was trying to write poems, while Deane was trying to write poetry.

That kind of recognition or support probably underpins what Heaney later called the first "living poetry environment" he found in Belfast. But what Heaney probably more specifically meant by that was the circle that formed in Belfast around the English poet Philip Hobsbaum. In London, Hobsbaum had been known as a member of The Group, a collection of poets who met regularly to read and comment on their poems. Hobsbaum conducted similar workshops in Belfast and Heaney, Michael Longley, James Simmons, and others took part in them.

By this time, Heaney had graduated from Queen's, earned a Teacher Training Diploma from St Joseph's College of Education in Belfast, taught at St Thomas' Intermediate School where Michael McLaverty, a fiction writer, was headmaster, and then returned to St Joseph's as a teacher.

Signs of this contact with a "living poetry environment" turn up in a number of ways in Heaney's work. Some of the poems in *Death of a Naturalist* are dedicated to members of the poetry group. A memory of advice to the young poet from Michael McLaverty appears in a later poem, 'Singing School'. The connection with Philip Hobsbaum also led to Heaney's early publications outside Belfast. Hobsbaum sent some of the poems to Edward Lucie-Smith who, in turn, sent them to editors. Some of the poems appeared in the *New Statesman* and *The Listener*, and some were broadcast on the BBC. From the circle in Belfast lines went out that helped to establish a broader audience for Heaney's poetry.

These poets also took part in a Belfast Festival. A number of pamphlets of poems were published for the festival by members of the group along with Derek Mahon and Seamus Deane. Heaney's *Eleven Poems*, now a collector's item, was issued as one of these pamphlets. These connections and activities led to the publication of *Death of a Naturalist* by Faber and Faber in 1966. Faber was the most distinguished publishing house for poetry in Britain in those days. T.S. Eliot had been a director of the firm and Faber had published Philip Larkin's *The Whitsun Weddings* two years earlier.

As Heaney's first volume took shape, his private life changed. He married Marie Devlin in 1965. Their son, Michael, was born the next year – the year Heaney's first volume appeared. The volume is a youthful one but also expresses the wish for maturity. There is the sense that by becoming a father himself Heaney wished to set aside or modify the emphasis on himself as a son. In fact, that seems to be the book's organizing principle.

IV

Heaney retained only ten of the 34 poems in *Death of a Naturalist* when he prepared *Opened Ground: Poems 1966-1996*, restoring three poems that did not appear in his earlier *Selected Poems* – 'The Barn', 'Churning Day', and 'The Diviner'. These ten poems hang together while maintaining the shape of the original collection, opening with 'Digging' and closing with 'Personal Helicon'. The shape is fixed as a kind of poet's spiritual autobiography. The poems are redolent of childhood, country life, and nostalgia; and celebrate experiences of two springs of emotion: beauty and terror, love and death.

On re-reading the poems, I have the sense that, for better or worse, despite echoes and influences, Heaney needed to write these poems, that their best lines, if at times coarse or clumsy, are not the result of the poet's wish to write a poem, but rather forced themselves on the poet. Heaney himself has talked as if these lines were already in him and his job was simply to set them loose. The first eight lines of 'Churning Day' give a sense of what I mean. Such lines are not to everyone's taste, certainly. But the last four of these lines, even with their heavy onomatopoeia, move with an authority Heaney rarely achieves, an authority that does not come from his craft or determination but from inspirations:

> And in the house we moved with gravid ease,
> our brains turned crystals full of clean deal churns,
> the plash and gurgle of the sour-breathed milk,
> the pat and slap of small spades on wet lumps.

The poems Heaney left out of *Opened Ground* are of a very different type or, rather, types. They consist of anecdotes of life in Belfast, love poems, reflections on the potato famine of 1845, and literary references to Joyce, Synge, and Saint Francis. What they have in common is that they spring from Heaney's uncertainty, from his ability and wish to manufacture poems when he is not compelled to do so. The result, often, is not so much bad poems as dead matter, something that isn't poetry at all:

> Stinking potatoes fouled the land,
> pits turned pus into filthy mounds:
> and where potato diggers are,
> you still smell the running sore.

It is difficult to believe this quatrain from 'At a Potato Digging' was written by the same person who wrote, "And in the house we moved with gravid ease". It is no doubt true, in one way, that they were not written by the same person. 'Churning Day' was written by Seamus Heaney. 'At a Potato Digging' was written by 'Seamus Heaney' also known as 'Famous Seamus', the person who had the skill, the "craft and determination", to write things editors would publish and critics would make much of even when he was not moved to say anything at all, even when he was 'uninspired'. From the beginning, there was this conflict between the Heaney of uncertainty and the Heaney with authority.

What this quatrain represents is a piece of rhetoric, worked up after reading Cecil Woodham-Smith and Patrick Kavanagh, using strong language to mask the absence of strong feeling. The poem is mechanically rather than organically organized, juxtaposing past and present in a way that is meant to suggest profundity rather than being profound. Worse, 'At a Potato Digging' is the only poem in *Death of a Naturalist* that is divided into sections identified by roman numerals and arranged as a sequence. There is a pretentiousness about this that the other poems in the book lack. They are content to be individual lyric poems. 'At a Potato Digging' is the first attempt at a mini-epic, a trying on of the bardic robes that Heaney felt obliged to wear, although as Ian Hamilton has pointed out there is something charming about the awkwardness and diffidence with which he has worn them. The most disconcerting thing about the poem is that Heaney becomes most longwinded when he has least to say, an inauspicious omen.

The fact is that Heaney had too few true poems, poems that grew from an inner necessity, to fill his first volume. It is almost true to say that, as a result, the book is a beginning and an end separated by a muddle. The muddle arises from literary ambition, the prize-winning grind deciding on poetry as a career. The muddle consists of an almost frenetic taking up of themes and styles that, in the end, largely results in fill that expands ten poems into a volume.

This is not at all to say that the fill is without interest or has failed to attract readers. 'The Early Purges' has become widely assigned in schools, for instance. Heaney reports that he set it aside because the poem's back now seems to him broken by a shift in voice. The title is ironic and the poem's form is a Heaneyfied version of Dante's *terza rima*. It opens with a memory of childhood, of kittens being drowned by a playmate. What is central to the poem is the poet's reaction to the drowning, to an early acquaintance with death. His reaction, understandably, is one of fear. The voice then shifts because the poet is now ostensibly speaking from the perspective of an adult present rather than from the perspective of a childish past:

> "Prevention of cruelty" talk cuts ice in town
> Where they consider death unnatural,
> But on well-run farms pests have to be kept down.

There is a false bravado about this that is reminiscent of the "snug as a gun" of 'Digging'. It is as if a bookish, sensitive, literary man catches himself appearing bookish, sensitive, and literary in public and he wishes to exorcise the image. The result is a literary effort that rings false, an echo of Larkin's "Books are a load of crap", without Larkin's humour.

What, in the end, is most promising about *Death of a Naturalist* is 'Poem' and 'Personal Helicon', the poem with which the volume concludes. Both of these suggest Heaney might find a way to continue writing poems that will be true to his original impulse without merely becoming repetitive or producing parodies of his most characteristic work. The first, inscribed "For Marie", is written to his wife – making the "you" of the poem an actual person rather than the anonymous and multitudinous "you" addressed in 'At a Potato Digging'. The four neat, unpretentious quatrains of 'Poem' work a transformation similar to the one worked in 'Digging'. There is less strain involved in this transformation, however, because it is worked by love rather than labour. The first and last stanzas show the nature of the transformation:

> Love, I shall perfect for you the child
> Who diligently potters in my brain
> Digging with heavy spade till sods were piled
> Or puddling through muck in a deep drain.

and

> Love, you shall perfect for me this child
> Whose small imperfect limits would keep breaking:
> Within new limits now, arrange the world
> Within our walls, within our golden ring.

To my mind, this last line was written by the Heaney with authority. The Heaney who suffers from uncertainty later revised it, making it more intellectually clever but less heartfelt by eliminating its apt repetitions and the fitting use of the plural possessive, "our": "And square the circle: four walls and a ring." Like John Crowe Ransom, a poet with whom Heaney has other traits in common, he was capable of turning the gold of a naturally magical line into the fool's gold of a magical-sounding line through revision. 'Personal Helicon' is inscribed "For Michael Longley," one of his fellow Belfast poets and a part of his earliest "living environment of poetry". The title might be a little forbidding. Oh, no, we might think, here comes another poem about being a poet. But the title is ironic and the simplicity and honesty of the first line force us to set any such concerns aside: "As a child, they could not keep me from wells". The first four of the poem's five quatrains describe the poet's childish fascination with wells and the growths, animals, sights, and sounds associated with them. Rats seems to have held a peculiar terror for Heaney and one brings his recollections to an abrupt ending here.

The rudely interrupted vision brings on the statement of the final stanza, the announcement of how Heaney hopes to continue as a poet:

> Now, to pry into roots, to finger slime,
> To stare, big-eyed Narcissus, into some spring
> Is beneath all adult dignity. I rhyme
> To see myself, to set the darkness echoing.

This statement at the end of the last poem in *Death of a Naturalist* is not incompatible with the conclusion of 'Digging', the first poem in the book – "I'll dig with it." Both express the urge to continue with the desires and preoccupations of childhood but in a metaphorical way, a kind of sublimation if you will. These desires and preoccupations are the desires and preoccupations of a "naturalist" – dirty, muddy, slimy, terrifying as well as fruitful, frightening as well as productive. Nonetheless, Heaney sees them here as his proper subject, a subject that will allow him to continue to see himself and to set the darkness echoing, two ways of reassuring himself of his present existence and the continuing existence of his voice after his death. These might seem like odd aims to people in other fields, but they are legitimate and necessary aims for a poet. In expressing them,

Heaney used his own distinctive and natural voice.

Publication of *Death of a Naturalist* in 1966 catapulted Seamus Heaney into fame before he had reached the age of thirty. The book was, by and large, generously welcomed by reviewers and was awarded prizes. Heaney joined the staff of Queen's University as a lecturer, filling the slot that opened when Philip Hobsbaum left. It no doubt looked as if he would continue in Belfast as a teacher and a poet as some of his own teachers had done. On the other hand, the reactions to the first book were such that they could well have encouraged him to consider pursuing poetry as a full-time profession.

In any case, some change in Heaney took place, at least in the eyes of Seamus Deane who, as a student at Cambridge University, had not seen Heaney for some years and never directly played a part in the literary activity in Belfast:

> He had just been married, and he arrived with his wife, Marie, bearing a copy of his first book, *Death of a Naturalist*, news of a prize that went with it, and, wonder of wonders, a bottle of whiskey. Heaney the teetotaller had gone. Heaney the poet had arrived.

Part of the reason for the enthusiastic reception of *Death of a Naturalist* is made clear by Christopher Ricks' review of it in the *New Statesman*. Ricks' first sentence reads: "Literary gentlemen who remain unstirred by Seamus Heaney's poems will simply be announcing that they are unable to give up the habit of disillusionment with recent poetry." What this sentence indicates is that the audience for poetry in Britain in 1966 consisted primarily of "literary gentlemen" reviewers, who had become disillusioned with recent poetry.

This needs explanation. Following the death of Dylan Thomas in 1953 there had been a reaction against the magic of language in poetry, word-play, puns, and so on. Philip Larkin and the poets of the so-called Movement were seen by some as dry, ironic, and rational. The disillusionment with poetry seems to have been based on the conviction that contemporary poetry must necessarily be either obscure or dull, if not both. A renewed interest in the poetry of Robert Graves and the emergence of Ted Hughes were then seen by some as positive signs. Others thought that confessional poetry, primarily American, might offer contemporary poetry a new lease on life. Ricks argued that Heaney all but single-handedly blew aside the thick clouds of obscurity and dullness that had cast poetry in their disillusioning shade:

> The deploying of rhymes and half-rhymes, the subtle taking up of hints, the sardonic pitying puns – there can be no doubt about Mr Heaney's technical fertility, and it gains its reward in a directness, a freedom from all obscurity, which is yet resonant and uncondescending.

It was this marriage of technical skill and freedom from obscurity that made reviewers welcome Heaney. The technical skill provided evidence of seriousness. The lack of obscurity allowed for accessibility and an emotional response. After the dryness of the Movement and the idiosyncratic whispering of the confessional poets, Heaney's verbal richness, clarity, and emotion hit readers of poetry with the effect of a rainstorm after drought. It was as if a new Dylan Thomas had arrived and people this time knew what he was talking about.

Ricks had the generosity to concentrate on Heaney's best poems – "His best poems are a delight, and as a first collection *Death of a Naturalist* is outstanding." Ricks was also good at telling which of the poems were best and why. He quotes from or discusses 'Digging', 'Follower', 'The Diviner', 'Churning Day', 'Death of a Naturalist', 'The Barn', and 'Blackberry-Picking', all of which are included in the ten poems from the volume that Heaney continues to collect. With reference to the two-thirds of the book that I have described as fill, Ricks contents himself to assert "The two poems on Ireland's great hunger are masterly", without quoting from either poem or attempting to make a case for the assertion, and to suggest, "Only in some of the love poems is there a note of mimicry (Robert Graves?)".

It is clear that Ricks was generous in part because of his own willingness to be stirred by the poems and his wish to overcome the disillusionment with contemporary poetry – both understandable aims. But Heaney might have benefited more if Ricks had not only praised his best work but also cautioned him about the nature and quality of the other things he had published. After all, 'Twice Shy', perhaps one of the love poems Ricks had in mind, uses an overtly literary metaphor to warn against lovers showing their feelings too soon, and in language that is condescending and nonresonant:

> Our juvenilia
> Had taught us both to wait,
> Not to publish feeling
> And regret it all too late –
> Mushroom loves already
> Had puffed and burst in hate.

Ricks and other reviewers certainly could have encouraged Heaney to learn to wait while praising those true poems that had come to him while he waited. Ian Hamilton can be said to have sounded a warning when, using the pen name 'Peter Marsh', he described the book as a "strange featureless first collection."

Heaney's mature view of *Death of a Naturalist* is fair enough, if we think of the book as ten poems rather than thirty-four: "*Death of a Naturalist* is a book of initiation, discovery, pleasure, joy, saying, 'Oh gosh, this can be done, and maybe I can blow a few notes of my own.' It's all 'big-eyed Narcissus', as it says at the end of the book." The trouble is that Heaney did not stop there. He added a statement that shows he had not learned to wait but rather was anxious to keep moving, to take on a more public, bardic role: "But almost immediately, I said to myself, 'You must move from I to we – open it out somehow.'" This advice, this active planning of the next book, this sense of poetry as a career, a series of steps to be followed, of moves to be made, is an expression of Heaney's uncertainty. The expression of Heaney's authority is much more modest:

> Love, you shall perfect for me this child
> Whose small imperfect limits would keep breaking.

2

Door into the Dark and *Wintering Out*

There is not a single sonnet in *Death of a Naturalist*. This is surprising when you consider Heaney's technical virtuosity and what his literary masters – Hopkins, Frost, Dylan Thomas, and Wordsworth – did with the sonnet. It is especially surprising when you consider what Heaney himself eventually did with the form. In any event, the title of his second book *Door into the Dark*, published in 1969, is drawn from a sonnet, 'The Forge'.

I

'The Forge' is one of a number of poems by Heaney that celebrates a craft that is going out of fashion, that is part of a way of life that is passing if not past. There can be little doubt that Heaney means for these crafts to stand as figures for poetry, but he rarely makes the comparison explicit. The result is a heightened objectivity that could be related to his wish to move from 'I' to 'we'. The 'I' is certainly present in 'The Forge', but after the first line – "All I know is a door into the dark." – it serves merely to record sensations.

As with the best poems in *Death of a Naturalist*, 'The Forge' uses rhyme – sometimes idiosyncratically – and relies on a rhythm that is related to the 'sprung rhythm' of Gerard Manley Hopkins. The sensory impressions are strong and the observation of detail is acute. The content of the poem, too, suggests a healthy recognition of the limits of 'craft and determination', of conscious knowledge, in the making of poetry. The first line is the expression of the poet's conscious, listening for hints and suggestions from the unconscious forge where poems are made.

The smith who works the forge, however, is not simply a figure for the poet's unconscious, but a separate character:

> He leans out on the jamb, recalls a clatter
> Of hoofs where traffic is flashing in rows;

In other words, we are again presented with the poet remembering someone who is remembering, recalling. The poem is an act of memory that celebrates memory. In this way, it can be read as a continuation of the intention expressed in 'Digging'. If the verbal pyrotechnics of 'The Forge' are subdued, controlled, it represents honest anvil work that at times yields an "unpredictable fantail of sparks".

'Thatcher' is a kind of companion piece to 'The Forge'. It again celebrates a craft that is intended as a figure for poetry. In this poem, the 'I' disappears completely, becomes a 'he', with the 'I' merely implied as the observer and recorder, a watching child or the 'objective' poet. The poem, however, is again an act of memory – it is written in the past tense – and the implied 'I' of the poem is expressed in the poem's form.

'Thatcher' consists of four quatrains made up of near-rhyming couplets – "morning/slung", "knives/eaves", and "blades/rods" are examples of the sounds at the ends of lines that bind the couplets together. The rhythm is again 'sprung', relying primarily on ten-syllable lines that in the first two quatrains rarely fall into iambic pentameter but become more firmly iambic in the last two quatrains. This shift in the poem's rhythm accompanies a shift in the poem's sense and, I suspect, a shift that took place during the composition of the poem, making the 'he' and the implied 'I' of the poem one.

The first two quatrains describe the thatcher turning up

"unexpectedly" at a home that needs a new roof, checking the old roof, preparing his tools and materials and, as the poet concludes in the last line of the second quatrain: "It seemed he spent the morning warming up". This line of iambic pentameter concludes the warm up for the poet as well as the thatcher and both set to work in the next quatrain.

The final stanza is meant to have the effect on the reader that the completed roof has on the occupants of the house:

> Couchant for days on sods above the rafters,
> He shaved and flushed the butts, stitched all together
> Into a sloped honeycomb, a stubble patch,
> And left them gaping at his Midas touch.

There is something breathtaking about this final quatrain, but that breathtaking quality is not the frisson associated with being in the presence of poetry so much as the "gaping" associated with witnessing an extraordinary performance. A sign of the 'performance' quality of the quatrain is the introduction of alien matter – "Couchant" and "Midas touch" – into this work that otherwise consists of a verbal web of hazel and willow rods. Another sign of this 'performance' quality is the closing shift from 'he' to 'them' – the owners of the house, the Heaney family possibly, but also readers, Heaney's growing audience.

'Thatcher' is certainly among Heaney's best poems. But the poem helps us to understand why, as Ian Hamilton reports, people find Heaney's work "teachable" rather than "memorable". The theme and technical virtuosity make 'Thatcher' a 'masterpiece' in the original meaning of that word: it is presented as proof that Heaney has served his poetic apprenticeship, hit the road as a journeyman, and is now ready to be certified as a master, free to set up shop on his own. The problem, of course, is that poetry is not only a craft or art, a skill within the control of the poet, the result of industry. Poetry also relies on something outside the poet's control – call it 'inspiration' if you like, or a "psychic disturbance", as the poet James Reeves put it, if you prefer.

The 'Midas touch', it must be remembered, was a curse, a punishment for an excessive and single-minded desire for gold, wealth. While having that touch might cause others to gape, it also kills what its possessor loves. Although the 'I', the ego of the poet literally disappears from 'Thatcher', he is in fact omnipresent: he is the thatcher and the 'them' who admire the thatcher's work. 'Thatcher' is a breathtaking but loveless performance.

'The Peninsula' is explicitly about a failure of inspiration, about what to do "when you have nothing more to say". The answer is to go for a drive around "the peninsula". The point of the drive is that "you will not arrive/But pass through", which sounds like a way for Heaney to keep going as a poet even though when he returns home from the drive it will still be with "nothing to say". The verse reaches its height in the third of this poem's four quatrains, a quatrain introduced with the phrase "Now recall", by now a kind of charm for Heaney:

> The glazed foreshore and silhouetted log,
> That rock where breakers shredded into rags,
> The leggy birds stilted on their own legs,
> Islands riding themselves out into the fog,

This is fine handiwork, of course, but it remains the work of a poet who has nothing to say and goes for a drive to find something to say and, admittedly, fails to do so. It might be better for a poet to say nothing when he has nothing to say, but that silence seems to be beyond Heaney. Perhaps he literally needs to write to assure himself of his continuing existence as he suggested in 'Personal Helicon'. In any case, it is the uncertain Heaney who writes poems like 'The Peninsula'.

Some critics argue that Heaney was forced by events in Northern Ireland to deal with political matters in his poetry. Heaney in the interview with Karl Miller rejects this idea, stating that he placed this demand on himself, and relating it to his desire to move from 'I' to 'we'. One of his earliest overtly political poems is 'Requiem for the Croppies', a sonnet in *Door into the Dark* in which the poet uses 'we' by speaking for the dead. According to Helen Vendler, this sonnet, through its title, represents a response to Geoffrey Hill's 'Requiem for the Plantagenet Kings'. This reminds us that Heaney's early poems were pastiches and that reading, as well as going for drives, might be a way he seeks the impulse to write, that is, when he "spends the morning warming up".

Heaney himself has stated that he wrote the poem in 1966 as a way to commemorate the anniversary of the Easter Rebellion of 1916. It is characteristic of him that he did not write about the Easter Rebellion but instead found what he thought of as an historical analogy for it – an earlier revolutionary movement during which the English army killed Irish soldiers at Vinegar Hill in County Wexford in 1798.

It is unclear why Heaney relies so heavily on analogies. They are in a way, of course, extended metaphors and can therefore be thought of as an extension of the poet's role as an image maker. In logic, however, while analogies can be useful, they inevitably break down and, as a result, must be used with caution. One weakness in their use is that they can cause confusion rather than clarity. In this case, would many readers realise that Heaney's sonnet was meant to commemorate the anniversary of Easter 1916? Beyond that, Heaney himself reports that the meaning of the poem changed as the situation in Northern Ireland changed. He originally intended it as a "silence-breaker", he says, as an attempt to "make a space, as we'd say now, for a nationalist cultural, political position. To make an intervention in the official public speech and discourse of Northern Ireland ..." In time, this relatively benign and potentially healthy purpose turned nasty. " ... I have to admit that the poem's meaning changed over the years. By the mid-Seventies, to recite 'Requiem for the Croppies' in Ireland in public would have been taken as a gesture of solidarity with the Provisionals." In other words, he concludes, the poem "would have turned into a propaganda tool." Heaney tends to be very careful when he makes statements such as this one. But I think he minimises the extent of the poem's possible use as "a propaganda tool". If publicly recited in Glasgow, Manchester, London, Toronto, Boston, Philadelphia, San Francisco, or Sydney in the mid-seventies, the poem could have struck at least some listeners as "a gesture of solidarity with the Provisionals."

Mostly the poem records Heaney's penchant for a way of life that is gone, his nostalgia for a simpler, rural past. His picturing of the Croppies dying "shaking scythes at cannon" is roughly equivalent to the blacksmith of 'The Forge' recalling "a clatter/Of hoofs where traffic is flashing in rows". What is relatively new in this sonnet is an almost explicit use of a vegetation myth of resurrection, an anthropological expression of a political sense:

> They buried us without shroud or coffin
> And in August the barley grew up out of the grave.

The last line echoes the first – "The pockets of our greatcoats full of barley" – in a way that is designed to be memorable.

Heaney suggests there was something subversive about this use of the sonnet form. The use of an 'official' English form to embody subcultural material – the ballads on 1798 he had heard as a boy – for him constitutes a kind of transgression. In fact, the ghost behind this sonnet is Milton, the puritan republican who used the sonnet for public purposes.

'Bogland' is the poem in *Door into the Dark* that Heaney points to as representative of his move from 'I' to 'we', a change of pronoun that he means to be symbolic of a shift from the private to the public, from boyhood to maturity, and from personal subject matter to "the matter of Ireland." It is the kind of poem that appeals to some critics because it allows them to track the poet's 'development'. The manner shifts as well as the matter but, to my mind, it does not represent an 'advance'.

The poem consists of seven unrhymed quatrains in a rhythm

that relies on two or three accents to the line and approaches a controlled free verse. It is a descriptive and reflective poem, describing a landscape and reflecting on its past. The poem also shows the poet's growing interest in anthropology and archaeology. One indication that 'Bogland' is the work of the uncertain Heaney is the third quatrain, what can be read as an unintentionally funny description of the poet's rapidly-growing public persona:

> They've taken the skeleton
> Of the Great Irish Elk
> Out of the peat, set it up,
> An astounding crate full of air.

II

In 1968, the year before *Door into the Dark* was published, Heaney's second son, Christopher (named for the poet's brother who had died as a child, a death commemorated in 'Mid-Term Break' in *Death of a Naturalist*), was born, and the marches on behalf of the civil rights of Catholics in Northern Ireland began. It was difficult, if not impossible, for a young intellectual to remain apolitical in 1968 – the year of the Prague spring, of the rising of students and workers in Paris, and the massive demonstrations against the war in Vietnam in the United States and elsewhere. Heaney's work did not become overtly political rapidly, however. *Wintering Out*, published in 1972, can be seen as a continuation of *Door into the Dark*.

The book's title is a phrase from 'Servant Boy', a little narrative poem based on a character who is part of a way of life that is past, as is 'Thatcher', but cast in a more 'open form', in some ways reminiscent of 'Bogland'. There is again an explicit relationship established between the speaker of the poem and the title character of it – "how/you draw me into/your trail". It is as if Heaney has lost his way and is rummaging through the past in search of guidance.

It is neither surprising nor shameful if Heaney felt at a loss. He was a Catholic in Northern Ireland writing in English with a growing audience of English and American as well as Irish readers. He had received the Somerset Maugham Award and as a result spent some months in Europe in 1969. At the same time, he felt this desire or requirement to become a public poet, using 'we' rather than 'I'. It was a situation designed to leave anyone who faced it squarely at a loss – at once pulled in a number of directions while wishing to go his own way and unsure, uncertain, what his own way was.

Place names play a more prominent part in *Wintering Out* than crafts do. Anahorish, the location of Heaney's first school, moves him to a reverie on the name that has a lyric simplicity. But these place names are also a way for Heaney to deal with the divisions and conflicts in Ireland as in 'Broagh':

> ended almost
> suddenly, like that last
> *gh* the strangers found
> difficult to manage.

Such poems continue to display Heaney's interest in language and display real verbal skill if the energy level is low. The absence of a personal pronoun for the speaker of the poem gives 'Broagh' an impersonal quality that again accounts for its being teachable rather than memorable. Similar subject matter is enlivened when it is once again made personal, as in 'A New Song'. It is not necessary to identify the 'I' of this poem with the poet. 'A New Song' in fact has the anonymous quality of a traditional ballad. But the poet's willingness to speak in a personal way, to use the first person singular, is enough to give the material added life.

Wintering Out constitutes what might be called a 'transitional volume'. 'The Tollund Man' suggests one kind of work Heaney will primarily pursue in the future and 'Good-night' shows him revisiting the roots of his original poetic impulse.

In 1969, Faber and Faber published P.V. Glob's *The Bog People*, a book by a Danish archaeologist on bodies of ritual murder victims from the Iron Age that had been preserved by peat bogs in Denmark. Heaney's reaction to the book's photographs was immediate and strong: "The unforgettable photographs of these victims blended in my mind with photographs of atrocities, past and present, in the long rites of Irish political and religious struggles." What these photographs set off in Heaney was his characteristic propensity for finding analogies. Just as he could celebrate the fiftieth anniversary of the Easter Rising with a sonnet on the Croppies, he could lament historic and contemporary Irish atrocities by writing about the bog people of Iron Age Denmark, beginning with 'The Tollund Man'.

The poem opens with a decision to go on a quest or pilgrimage:

> Some day I will go to Aarhus
> To see his peat-brown head,
> The mild pods of his eyelids,
> His pointed skin cap.

This poem juxtaposes past and present in much the same way that 'At a Potato Digging' did. It is also organised as a sequence consisting of three sections set off with roman numerals. The first section consists of this wish to see the Tollund Man and an identification of the poet with the victim of a ritual murder in terms that are reminiscent of Robert Graves' *The White Goddess*, 'Bridegroom to the goddess'. The second section connects the Tollund Man with political murders in Ireland in the early 1920s: "The scattered, ambushed/Flesh of labourers,/ Stockinged corpses/Laid out in the farmyards." The third and final section returns to an identification of the poet with the Tollund Man:

> Out there in Jutland
> In the old man-killing parishes

> I will feel lost,
> Unhappy and at home.

A contemplation of photographs of the ritually slaughtered in Iron Age Denmark allowed Heaney to say how he felt about living in Northern Ireland in the late 1960s and early 1970s – "lost,/Unhappy and at home".

Oddly enough, although 'Good-night' has much more in common with Heaney's early work than with 'The Tollund Man', it is extremely objective, the 'I' of the poem merely implied. More than that, this objectivity is a cause of mystery. It is not at all clear exactly who the "they" or the "she" of the poem are. The language of the poem's two quatrains is simple and the poem's concluding line comes with an inevitability that suggests it was a surprise to the poet as it is to the reader: "And cancels everything behind her." Despite its mystery, obscurity, 'Good-night' bears the stamp of Heaney's poetic authority. 'The Tollund Man', despite its clarity, its use of analogy, springs from Heaney's uncertainty. It is that uncertainty that finds its fullest expression in Heaney's next book, *North* (1975).

3

North and *Field Work*

Seamus Heaney published a collection of what might best be called prose poems entitled *Stations* in 1975. One of those prose poems, 'Incertus' shows that he early used the word as a pen name, a pseudonym, and explicitly deals with one side of Heaney's split nature: "Oh yes, I crept before I walked. The old pseudonym lies there like a mouldering tegument."

The pun on "lies" and the talk of a disguise suggest that Heaney felt, or wished to feel, able to leave his old uncertainty behind. That was unfortunate. His poetic authority depends on uncertainty – hints, suggestions, pushing forward by intuition and inspiration rather than by cocksure planning. *North*, Heaney's most controversial book, published in the same year as *Stations*, is also his most programmatic book, the one that most stridently attempts to shout down his uncertainty and strains to impress with the appearance of authority.

The trouble with *North* is not that it deals with 'The Troubles' in Northern Ireland after Heaney had moved south to County Wicklow in the Republic of Ireland, although it is his most directly political book. The trouble with the book instead is that the least satisfying elements in Heaney's work are given the upper hand in it – the bardic stance, the reliance on questionable historical analogies, and a kind of overweening arrogance that blinds the author to the presence of a tasteless self-indulgence in his work.

What provides the book with a saving grace is the fact that it is framed – opens and closes – with poems that display little or nothing of these traits and speak from the heart. These poems are 'Sunlight' and 'The Seed Cutters', two poems "in dedication" significantly entitled 'Mossbawn', a harking back to childhood and the family home, and 'Exposure', the poet's self-examination on trying to settle into his new home. The poems trace an arc from sunlight to nightfall and from seedtime to winter, suggesting that something has come to an end. Heaney has described his first four books as, in a way, one book, concluding with *North*; and that *Field Work* represents a new beginning.

I

The proper place of 'Sunlight' in Heaney's work is with the early poems of family life and of handicrafts that are implicitly metaphors for poetry. 'Sunlight' is a portrait of Heaney's aunt, Mary Heaney, defined by an absence – "There was a sunlit absence" – that fills with life through an act of memory, producing a perpetual presence:

> Now she dusts the board
> with a goose's wing,

Simple gestures described in simple language come to life as if by magic, through the combination of love and memory that is at the root of poetic expression. The poem concludes with a striking image that seems to recognise and sum up the relationship between the poet, his personal past, and his readers:

> And here is love
> like a tinsmith's scoop
> sunk past its gleam
> in the meal-bin.

The first person singular does not appear in this poem. The poet is present only by implication, a rememberer and a recorder. This self-effacing quality gives the poem its quiet authority.

The bulk of *North* is very different, based as it is on an analogy between the ritually slaughtered bog people of the Iron Age and 'The Troubles' of the late 1960s and early 1970s in Northern Ireland. The weakness of the method is made most clear in 'Punishment', in which a corpse found in a bog merges with a contemporary Irish woman punished for adultery. The poem consists of 11 four-line stanzas. The first five and a half of these describe the ancient corpse:

> I can see her drowned
> body in the bog,
> the weighing stone
> the floating rods and boughs.

In the concluding five and a half stanzas, the first person narrator – presumably the poet – addresses the contemporary adulteress and then describes the narrator's reaction to, position on, the "punishment" of the poem's title:

> I almost love you
> but would have cast, I know,
> the stones of silence.

This allusion to Jesus' way of dispersing the men who intended to stone a woman for adultery is a clue to Heaney's ambiguous reaction to what he describes. Stating that he would have cast stones means that he would have seen himself as free of sin, free to judge and condemn, free to punish. But the stones he claims he would have cast were not stones at all, rather stones of "silence". In other words, he would have been guilty of silently giving consent to the punishment, not speaking up to prevent it. The poem, it is suggested, is a breaking of that silence.

If left there, the sense of the poem, at least – setting the quality of the poem as a poem aside – might have been fair enough, the tortured sense of a humane witness to a contemporary horror. But Heaney did not leave the poem there. Instead, he felt obliged to define himself as an "artful voyeur" and went on to conclude:

I ...
who would connive
in civilized outrage
yet understand the exact
and tribal, intimate revenge.

Heaney's tendency to rely on historical analogies and to yoke opposites imply an equality between the two sides of the analogies and between the opposites he yokes. Here the "artful voyeur" would "connive in civilized outrage" and "yet understand ... revenge". This is not the statement of a tortured, conscience-stricken witness to a horror so much as that of someone sent into a kind of reverie by staring at a photograph in an archaeologist's book and finding in that reverie grist for an unfeeling, thoughtless mill.

Heaney has allowed, in an interview with Karl Miller, "Maybe it's the word 'tribal' that is wrong. 'Tribal' buys into the outsider's view of the conflict." Nevertheless, he reprinted the poem in *Opened Ground* without finding a better word, thus continuing to "buy into the outsider's view of the conflict". Heaney's whole analogical method, in fact, "buys into the outsider's view of the conflict" if by that he means the sense of senseless tribal vendettas. There are, of course, outsiders with a far more sophisticated view of the political struggles in Ireland than that. The tendency to generalise if not pontificate in Heaney repeatedly drives him to the use of clichés that inhibit or prevent thought.

It is insiders who have been most critical of *North* in any case. Heaney has described this criticism well but in terms that suggest he simply finds the criticism wrong-headed and that he takes a certain pride in having provoked it:

> ... I knew there was a kind of official policy on *North*, in the North. The statement of resistance to it came in a review by Ciaron Carson early on, but others took it up, and it has since been given a very thorough formulation. What they objected to, so they said, was what they saw to be the book's

aestheticisation of violence. The claim was that I had somehow bought into the notion that the violence that was happening in the North was a cyclic, fated, ongoing, predestined thing. I was simplifying and mythologising and aestheticising the violence, they felt. So there was a deep resistance.

This statement shows that Heaney can be an artful dodger as well as an artful voyeur. Just as he uses "would" in 'Punishment' to give the whole treatment a sense that he is dealing with a hypothetical rather than an actual situation, he here uses "so they said" and "what they objected to" to imply the critics of *North* are mistaken without saying that they are. If Heaney was not simplifying, mythologising, and aestheticising the violence in *North*, what he was doing is anybody's guess.

In the second section of *North*, the more directly contemporary section, Heaney includes 'Singing School', a long autobiographical sequence of poems on his poetic development as a Catholic in Northern Ireland. He opens the sequence with citations from Wordsworth's *The Prelude* and W.B. Yeats' *Autobiographies*. If there is irony in the use of these citations they nonetheless serve to show that Heaney is consciously making a bid to be considered a 'major poet'. This bid is implicit in the scheme and subject matter of 'Singing School' even without the citations. Why else would anyone take an interest in the biographical details of Heaney's development?

The poem in the sequence entitled 'Summer 1969' clearly shows the dangers of thinking in terms of 'major status' for a poet:

> While the Constabulary covered the mob
> Firing into the Falls, I was suffering
> Only the bullying sun of Madrid.

Such an opening suggests that Heaney was well aware that there was something comic about the terms in which he described his privileged position, the matter-of-fact description of life-and-death events in Ireland contrasted with the "suffering" he faced in Spain. In fact, the poem never directly returns to the events in Ireland at all but continues to take relatively seriously Heaney's plight as a young intellectual on holiday or on a grant in Spain, reading the biography of James Joyce and listening to friends advise him on his public role: "Go back," one said, "try to touch the people".

Retreating from the heat of the bullying sun to "the cool of the Prado", Heaney contemplates three paintings by Goya that imply three possible reactions to events in Ireland. The concluding lines seem to be a comment on Goya that is meant to convey how he might serve as a model for the public poet, a poet who feels called upon to comment on current political events:

> He painted with his fists and elbows, flourished
> The stained cape of his heart as history charged.

There is a hollow ring to these lines, a sense that the author is straining to produce an effect rather than achieving a sense of himself. The portrait of the artist as a young bullfighter is not only a cliché in itself, but a cliché of questionable taste when it comes soon after these lines:

> We sat through death-counts and bullfight reports
> On the television, celebrities
> Arrived from where the real thing happened.

The "death-counts" here refer to news of the war in Vietnam. It seems Heaney found it impossible to keep from simplifying and aestheticising the violence not only in Northern Ireland but everywhere in the world. Although he had early pledged to dig with his pen, the lingering adolescent sense of it being "snug as a gun" caused him merely to skim the televised surface of current events.

'Exposure', the concluding poem in 'Singing School', is very different from 'Summer 1969' although it deals with some of the same issues. One of the reasons Heaney moved with his family to the South, to County Wicklow, was to try and become a full-time writer, to stop teaching. As a result, he began to write a good deal more prose, journalism. While such a decision can be seen as a deepening commitment to poetry, this need to produce prose might help to account for the journalistic element in much of *North*. Some critics noticed that he often worked up the same material in both prose and verse. Still, 'Exposure', the first of Heaney's poems dealing with his transplantation, is not fundamentally journalistic:

> It is December in Wicklow:
> Alders dripping, birches
> Inheriting the last light,
> The ash tree cold to look at.

This first stanza serves to remind us Heaney did not only move from North to South but also from the city, Belfast, to the country. The cottage, called Glanmore, he inhabited with his family was in a way a return to Mossbawn, his starting point. But here in his new home he again worries about the why of his poetry, the nature of his role as a poet:

> How did I end up like this?
> I often think of my friends'
> Beautiful prismatic counselling
> And the anvil brains of some who hate me
>
> As I sit weighing and weighing
> My responsible *tristia*.
> For what? For the ear? For the people?
> For what is said behind-backs?

It is likely that, as some critics have argued, the reference to "*tristia*" here is an allusion to the Roman poet Ovid in exile. Such an allusion does nothing to enlarge or open out the series of rhetorical questions Heaney raises. Fortunately for Heaney – and his readers – the only answer to these questions is poetry, the kind of poetry Heaney is capable of rarely, the kind of poetry that allows him, despite his uncertainty, to speak with authority:

> Rain comes down through the alders,
> Its low conducive voices
> Mutter about let-downs and erosions
> And yet each drop recalls
>
> The diamond absolutes.

North received the W.H. Smith Award and the Duff Cooper Prize. If reviewers in Belfast found fault with the book, others in London and the United States hailed it. The American poet Robert Lowell described it as "a new kind of political poetry by the best Irish poet since W.B. Yeats". Its reception assured the growth of Heaney's international reputation.

II

The tone of *Field Work* (1979) is primarily elegiac. It is not only that some of the best poems in the book – 'The Strand at Lough Beg' and 'Casualty' – are elegies. The stance of the author seems to have softened, is marked by sadness rather than the wish to force suffering into an architectonic scheme. The wish to be a public poet seems to have become tempered by the lingering need to be a private one. The two roles merge more successfully in this volume than in any other.

There seem to be a number of reasons for this. First, Heaney had not only settled in the Republic of Ireland but also returned to teaching. Second, the American poet Robert Lowell became a friend of Heaney's and undoubtedly influenced him. As Ian Hamilton, a biographer of Lowell, noticed in *Field Work*, "Heaney sounds that 'heartbreak' note which Robert Lowell used to talk about. Maybe Lowell talked to him about it. *Field Work* has an elegy in memory of Lowell ('the master elegist'), and the two poets saw each other often during the mid-seventies." Finally, Heaney turned forty years old in the year

Field Work appeared and the shift in tone no doubt has an air of middle age about it.

'The Strand at Lough Beg' is an elegy for a cousin of Heaney's, Colum McCartney, who had been murdered. Despite the closeness of the relationship and Heaney's use of the first-person singular, this elegy, like many elegies, is a public, rhetorical poem. The use of a quotation from Dante to introduce the poem and the reference to Sweeney, that figure of the poet in Medieval Ireland, in the poem's early lines, weigh the work down with overtly literary overtones.

This literary quality of the work does not diminish its power so much as define its nature. There is the sense that Heaney now needs to place his work in a lengthy literary tradition, to use the literature of the past to try to find his bearings. The poem moves from these literary references to the recent past rapidly: "What blazed ahead of you? A faked roadblock?"

Heaney does not linger long at the imaginatively reconstructed crime scene. Instead, he goes back to when he and his cousin were young. This dip into the past allows Heaney to speak rhetorically, publicly, but movingly, the rhythm of the verse quickening and the purpose of the poem achieved through a merger of past and present.

Elegy is a form that suits Heaney's talents. It is meant to be public, rhetorical, and beautiful – a work of art, a piece of artifice – although touching on a deeply personal emotion – grief. Rhythm, rhyme, and imagery here work together to celebrate the loss of an individual life in a universal way. Each elegy is a lament for the human condition.

'Casualty', too, is literary, but in a very different way. There are no citations from Dante or references to Medieval Irish works here. It seems to me that Yeats' poem, 'The Fisherman', with its short rhyming lines and its wish to find or define an audience for the poet, is behind Heaney's poem. This is how Yeats begins:

> Although I can see him still,
> The freckled man who goes

To a grey place on a hill
In grey Connemara clothes
At dawn to cast his flies,
It's long since I began
To call up to the eyes
This wise and simple man.

And this is how Heaney introduces us to the subject of his
elegy, another fisherman:

He would drink by himself
And raise a weathered thumb
Towards the high shelf,
Calling another rum
And blackcurrant, without
Having to raise his voice.

Yeats' fisherman was imaginary, a wise and simple man "who
did not exist". Heaney's fisherman is depicted as an actual
acquaintance, killed by his own side for failing to keep a curfew,
who in some way serves to represent the audience Heaney would
like to reach:

But my tentative art
His turned back watches too:

If the fisherman mentioned poetry, the poet, "always politic/
And shy of condescension", turned "the talk to eels/Or lore of
the horse and cart/Or the Provisionals". The distance between
the poet and his audience is caused less by the poet's education
than by the poet's character. But the poet clings to the notion
that it is education that sets him apart.

The fisherman, a hard drinker, breaks a curfew imposed to
mourn thirteen dead in Derry, and the poet imagines him raising
a question that the poet in fact puts to himself:

How culpable was he
That last night when he broke
Our tribe's complicity?

'Now you're supposed to be
An educated man,'
I hear him say. 'Puzzle me
The right answer to that one.'

In the poem's third and final section, the two men become
virtually one and their trades, their crafts, intertwine, fishing
described as if it were poetry and both connected with freedom.

This potential unity of poet and fisherman has, of course,
been ended by the intervention of death, the murder of the
fisherman. The poet is left with nothing to do but ask the
impossible:

Dawn-sniffing revenant,
Plodder through midnight rain,
Question me again.

Heaney here uses an elegy to stage a debate with himself.
'Casualty' cries out for comparison with 'Punishment' in *North*.
The poet now is no "artful voyeur" but he remains unable to
answer questions about culpability and tribal complicity. The
wish to be questioned again does not at all suggest that he has
found an answer or even that he is likely to do so. Instead, it
simply expresses the wish to have the dialogue continue.

Perhaps the most fully satisfying poem in the volume is a
sonnet and an elegy that does not deal with 'The Troubles' but
rather harks back to Heaney's earliest manner. It seems to refer
to the pump in 'Sunlight' from *North* and could be meant as an
elegy for the poet's aunt, Mary Heaney, the dedicatee of that
poem. In any case, 'A Drink of Water' would not appear out of
place in *Death of a Naturalist* or *Door into the Dark*. The poem
relies heavily on near rhyme, its rhythm might be described as
'sprung', and it includes that early magical mantra of Heaney's,
"I recall".

Some critics of Heaney's work welcomed *Field Work* with
something like relief. If *North* had caused them concern, *Field
Work* reassured them. Ian Hamilton made the case this way:

Field Work, to my mind, is the book of Heaney's that we ought to keep in mind (how can we not?) when there are grumbles about "anonymity" or "suppression of the self". His 'moi' poems are all the stronger, all the more hard-won, it seems to me, not because they go against his notion of a tribal role but because – at their best – they don't: it's just that, in these poems, the 'I' lurks behind the 'we', and vice versa. And the elegy is, of course, the perfect form for such lurking, or entwining: an intimacy meant to be made public.

4

Heaney Astray: The Later Poems

In his lecture, 'The Government of the Tongue', Seamus Heaney drew attention to the fact that both T.S. Eliot and Osip Mandelstam in their very different ways turned to the work of Dante "at a moment of mid-life crisis". It is possible that Heaney found this fact interesting, if not something more, because he also turned to Dante at such a time. Heaney included his 'Ugolino', a translation from Dante, in *Field Work*. There are other signs of such a crisis in the book, particularly the poem 'The Guttural Muse'. It is a brief poem in which the poet recalls his response when he looked out of the window of a hotel room:

> A girl in a white dress
> Was being courted out among the cars:
> As her voice swarmed and puddled into laughs
> I felt like some old pike all badged with sores
> Wanting to swim in touch with soft-mouthed life.

Oddly enough, Heaney's numerous commentators have tended to be silent on this modest but unpleasantly powerful poem. In any case, it seems clear that the middle-aged Heaney's career had made him feel as if he had lost touch with life. What is more, he identified life with the muse or, at least, a muse – the guttural muse, the muse of the language of his birthplace. If Heaney himself and some of his critics hoped that *Field Work* would represent a new beginning, they have been disappointed. Instead, it represents the consolidation of a position that had been struggled for and achieved. What comes later is marked by an understandable if regrettable exhaustion. There are a number of signs of this.

In 1976, Heaney and his family moved to Dublin from the cottage in County Wicklow. In 1980, the year after *Field Work* appeared, he published a collection of his prose, *Preoccupations*. In that same year, he also published *Poems 1965-1975*, a summing up designed to reinforce the questionable notion that his first four books were in fact one book. In 1982, he became a professor at Harvard. Finally, the next volume Heaney published was not a new book of original poems but a translation from the Medieval Irish, *Sweeney Astray*. In this stretch of five or six years, the youthful poet, big-eyed Narcissus, was transmogrified into a middle-aged international cultural figure, squint-eyed Narcissus. The later poems are by and large the work of this figure – a dull, garrulous, humorless name dropper who writes and publishes far too much, a failure of the self-critical sense, never this poet's strong suit.

There can be no question that Heaney knows what true poems are and knows the conditions under which they are written. In fact, he seems to have made something of a scholarly study of these conditions, another sign of his uncertainty. In 'The Government of the Tongue', he cites the Polish poet Anna Swir on inspiration as a psychosomatic phenomenon; the ancient Greek notion that in a lyric poem "it is a god that speaks"; Rilke; and Robert Frost's memorable piece of prose, 'The Figure A Poem Makes'. But Heaney's paraphrase of Frost gives us a sample of his middle-aged, professorial voice: " … any interference by the knowing intellect in the purely disinterested cognitions of the form-seeking imagination constitutes poetic sabotage, an affront to the legislative and executive powers of expression itself." This trendy academic jargon, with its false opposition between intellect and imagination, combined with a trendy but misleading political analogy, is the statement of a poet for whom poetry is fast becoming either a memory or an object of study.

Heaney's next book of poems, *Station Island* (1984), shows an expansion of his earlier practice of dealing with the same material in both verse and prose. In fact, both the title of the lecture I've quoted from and the Greek notion of how a true lyric comes into being appear in the brief poem 'Stone from Delphi':

> To be carried back to the shrine some dawn
> when the sea spreads its far sun-crops to the south
> and I make a morning offering again:
> *that I may escape the miasma of spilled blood,*
> *govern the tongue, fear hybris, fear the god*
> *until he speaks in my untrammeled mouth.*

Heaney's characteristic near rhyming is present here, but the rhythm is tired, slack and tentative, until it finds its way to the traditional iambic pentameter of the concluding two lines. The final line has an undeniable power, but it is the premeditated power of rhetoric rather than the startling power of poetry. The poem explicitly expresses the longing for inspiration rather than being the compelled expression of an inspiration. Worse, the analogy that is the basis of the poem suggests this longing might be fulfilled through a ritual conducted by the poet.

Much of the verse in *Station Island* has the appearance of being written out of habit or professional obligation rather than inspiration, the true urge. Part of this sense arises from the subject matter – from 'Underground' with its memory of Heaney's honeymoon in London, to the lengthy title sequence in which the ghost of Colum McCartney, Heaney's cousin, complains of the beautiful elegy Heaney wrote for him ("you ... saccharined my death with morning dew"), to a series of poems written in the person of the Medieval Sweeney – the volume is retrospective. When Heaney selected poems from *Station Island* to include in *Opened Ground*, he added 'Villanelle for an Anniversary', a public poem and tribute to the founder of Harvard University that contains a single line that seems to sum up Heaney's state: "The future was a verb in hibernation".

It took strong feelings to bring this state to an end. Heaney's mother died in 1984; his father died in 1986. These deaths seem to have broken through the state of hibernation he had entered and caused him rapidly to write a sequence of sonnets, *Clearances*, that, although dedicated to the memory of his mother, celebrate both his parents in heartfelt, awkward language. The poems were gathered in *The Haw Lantern* (1987). In Number II of the sequence he pictures his mother's death as a family reunion, her return to the house of her father:

> It is Number 5, New Row, Land of the Dead,
> Where grandfather is rising from his place
> With spectacles pushed back on a clean bald head
> To welcome a bewildered homing daughter
> Before she even knocks. 'What's this? What's this?'
> And they sit down in the shining room together.

This moving reunion becomes even more moving when we learn, in VII, that the idea for it came from Heaney's father speaking to his dying wife. This sonnet also gives the sequence its title. The first eight lines of it read:

> In the last minutes he said more to her
> Almost than in all their life together.
> 'You'll be in New Row on Monday night
> And I'll come up for you and you'll be glad
> When I walk in the door ... Isn't that right?'
> His head was bent down to her propped-up head.
> She could not hear but we were overjoyed.
> He called her good and girl. Then she was dead,

The surprising, compelled speech of poetry is often related to a deeply-rooted psychic disturbance. Moments of inspiration do not come when we long for them or perform rituals but when we are struck dumb by overwhelming emotions tied to love and death. Heaney has never again written anything to compare with these rapidly composed sonnets. Instead, much of what he has written since has been readable but forgettable.

One good example of these is an almost imagistic poem, 'An August Night', from *Seeing Things* (1991). Accurate observation, imaginative imagery, plain language, and modesty are the virtues of this brief poem. But it is the imagery of it, rather than the thing itself, the language, that stays in the memory.

Another example. 'Mint', from *The Spirit Level* (1996), consists of four near-rhyming four-line stanzas that consider the plant of the title as a metaphor for increasing age:

> But, to be fair, it also spelled promise
> And newness in the back yard of our life
> As if something callow yet tenacious
> Sauntered in green alleys and grew rife.

Nothing to take the breath away here, certainly, but it leads Heaney to suggest the possibility of a late crop of poems: "My last things will be first things slipping from me". In the last stanza, however, it is as if Heaney worries his private ruminations will not do, are insufficient, and he tacks on a conclusion marked by the expression of political guilt:

> Let the smells of mint go heady and defenceless
> Like inmates liberated in that yard.
> Like the disregarded ones we turned against
> Because we'd failed them by our disregard.

This concluding stanza makes it seem unlikely that Heaney's last things will be first things slipping from him so much as manufactured things clinging to him.

Since the publication of *Opened Ground* in 1998, Heaney has issued an additional volume of poems, *Electric Light* (2001). The collection has a scrappy, thrown-together feel. It contains a number of elegies for other famous poets that are literary in the worst sense. 'Audenesque', dedicated to the memory of Joseph Brodsky, opens this way:

Joseph, yes, you know the beat.
Wystan Auden's metric feet
Marched to it, unstressed and stressed,
Laying William Yeats to rest.

'On His Work in the English Tongue' dedicated to the memory of Ted Hughes, concludes, as an essay or lecture by Heaney might, with a quotation from the Nobel Laureate Czeslaw Milosz. The poem 'To The Shade of Zbigniew Herbert' does far less for the memory of the Polish poet than Heaney's brief discussion in prose of Herbert's poem 'The Knocker' did. It is hard to set aside the thought that what motivates these poems is fame by association rather than the requisite combination of affection and grief. To see what is wrong with these poems it is only necessary to compare them with a quatrain from William Dunbar's *Lament for the Makers*:

He has blind Harry and Sandy Traill
Slain with his shower of mortal hail.
The flesh is bruckle, the fiend is slee –
Timor mortis conturbat me.

The dominant emotion of *Electric Light* seems to be a self-satisfaction that prevents, renders the poet incapable of, strong feeling. The first poem in the book, 'At Toomebridge', relies for significance on a mere naming of or pointing towards things that have been significant in Heaney's poetry:

Where the rebel boy was hanged in '98.
Where negative ions in the open air
Are poetry to me. As once before
The slime and silver of the fattened eel.

This little, non-Homeric catalogue seems to be issued with a suppressed yawn and it might well induce yawns in readers. This sense of self-satisfaction reaches its peak in 'Known World', in which memories of and notebook entries from attendance at the Struga Poetry Festival in Yugoslavia in 1978 are combined with a memory of catching flies with flypaper in Northern Ireland in the 1950s and thoughts of refugees from the war in the Balkans, only to conclude with a self-portrait of the poet as cultural jet-setter:

> As the Boeing's innards trembled and we climbed
> Into the pure serene and protocols
> Of Air Traffic Control, courtesy of Lufthansa,
> I kept my seat belt fastened as instructed,
> Smoked the minute the No Smoking sign went off
> And took it as my due when wine was poured
> By a slight *de haut en bas* of my headphoned head.
> *Nema problema. Ja.* All systems go.

If Heaney's last things are to be first things, it now seems most likely that he will revert to those very first poems described by Seamus Deane and Heaney himself as pastiches rather than to the fresh if derivative beginnings of *Death of a Naturalist*. *Electric Light* should be enough to make even Heaney's most ardent admirers wish that he would learn to sit patiently in silence unless the god happens to speak in his untrammelled mouth.

5

Reputation and Achievement

"Famous Seamus," as Clive James put it, or "Seamus Heaney", with the ironic quotation marks Seamus Deane used more than a quarter of a century ago, is not, of course, the man who sits alone to write a poem, or boards an airplane in Dublin for Boston, or goes with his wife to stay at the cottage in Wicklow they once rented and now own. I think of "Famous Seamus" as one of those huge, comic, grotesque rubber creatures, filled with helium, that float above the crowds at the Macy's Thanksgiving Day parade in New York each year. People necessarily point and gape at the things because of their sheer size. But sensitive children are frequently frightened by them and if, as happened several years ago, one of the unwieldy things accidentally slips its moorings and gets loose, it can spread real terror – lumbering into passersby, knocking over hot dog stands, stopping traffic, and causing a mad scramble to retrieve and restrain the thing.

Seamus Heaney, the man and the poet, is not "Famous Seamus" – but there is a relationship between the two. It is as if the inflated, synthetic reputation is tentatively moored to a belt loop of the man himself.

I said at the outset that I thought this disparity between Heaney's reputation and his achievement could be attributed to a fundamental conflict in his nature, a peculiar combination of uncertainty and authority. His uncertainty seems to require, perhaps demands, the reassurance of external recognition – reviews, prizes, public attention, in short, contemporary fame.

His authority, on the other hand, springs from a slight but true poetic gift that is the source of some good poems, lines, and phrases. Whether this slight but true gift would have been more fruitful if it had been more carefully husbanded and not prematurely exposed to the glaring sun of publicity is now beside the point. In any case, these things are rarely a matter of choice and it is unlikely that Heaney could have done other than he did.

Some critics have insisted that Heaney should not be 'blamed' for his inflated reputation. Heaney himself in an interview has complained of the burden of being a media "phenomenon". The fact is, he tends to be mostly congratulated on his celebrity; and it seems grudging of him to complain of it publicly while adding to it. The real harm it causes is its distortion of the nature of his own achievement and of the nature of poetry in general. Somewhere along the line – perhaps at about the time when he wrote 'The Guttural Muse' and thought of himself as something of a sick fish – he seems to have mistaken what the Harvard philosopher William James called the "bitch-goddess success" for what Heaney at times calls the muse.

Mere bulk – the result of industry – might be a way to measure success, but it is irrelevant if not anathema to poetry. The way Heaney set about making his first book shows his willingness (if not his need) to care more about quantity than quality if the result would be publication, external recognition. The fill he was willing to use in that first book was the first blast of helium that went into the balloon of his reputation. And what was the result? Rave reviews, prizes, grants. More blasts of helium for the balloon. It would take a rare person indeed – and certainly not a young, ambitious poet suffering from uncertainty – to turn his back on the offered rewards and take a different course. Instead, he stayed the course and the result has been not only the Nobel Prize for Literature in 1995 but also the sight of his translation of *Beowulf* (1999) listed by the *New York Times* as an example of unread best-sellers. That points to the kind of distortion contemporary fame works. The writings of the famous become objects of trade, commodities to be purchased and owned but not read, much less re-read, loved, and remembered. In mythic terms, there is a poetic justice in this, the appropriate vengeance taken by the muse on devotees of the bitch-goddess success.

This is not at all to say that Heaney is alone responsible for his reputation, although there is something funny and accurate about a reviewer's comment that Heaney's only muse is his own fame. The fact of Heaney's early meeting with Helen Vendler in 1975 and her subsequently championing his work repeatedly in print – going so far as to close her book on him by accusing critics who have attacked his work of being motivated by political or social concerns rather than poetic ones – and others like it also do not explain the phenomenon of his popularity, his wide and international reputation. Literary log-rolling has been with us always – or, at least, for a few hundred years in its current form – but it has rarely been capable of such extravagant results. Instead, there must be something in the false consciousness of our age that finds Heaney's work congenial. What could that be?

My guess is it is the widespread sense of severed roots that results in a hunger for a romanticised, simplified past expressed in a contemporary, sophisticated way. Peter Dale caught the right note early when he reviewed *Death of a Naturalist* in *Agenda*: "Seamus Heaney writes of rustic matters and gives them a touch of modernity by using a vivid imagery gathered from modern warfare." But Heaney's work appeals to the contemporary hunger for the past and rootedness not only in subject matter and imagery. The technical virtuosity for which he has often been praised – even if it is at times little more than a cloyingly obvious onomatopoeia or a parody of his own early work – suggests an ancient, admirable craft modernised, brought up to date. The Bardic stance merely represents the apotheosis of this anachronistic position.

Heaney's success is, in a way, equivalent to the popularity of *Riverdance* – traditional Irish folk dancing, tricked out in sexy costumes and accompanied by electric guitars, goes to Broadway, but without the real excitement the dancers stir in audiences. The things he has chosen to translate – *Sweeney Astray* and *Beowulf* – are of a piece with this, epics from an 'heroic' past modernised, made contemporary. "Beowulf our contemporary," one reviewer shouted. Sweeney our contemporary. Dante our contemporary. It is as if the present is a poetic vacuum and so we soothe ourselves by luxuriating in the illusion the past is a perpetual now. A very different popular view of the barbarous past was expressed before the two World Wars in Mark Twain's *A Connecticut Yankee at King Arthur's Court*. Technology weakens the sense of space and time, making for an homogenised global culture that nonetheless projects the illusion that the local is everywhere, fostering anachronistic ethnic, religious, and national disputes, and that time – or at least history – has stopped, fostering fads and fashions without the need to produce anything new.

Poems that are alive – and therefore have the chance to live – resist the false consciousness of their time, are born with a built-in resistance to it. They discover and utter truths – small truths, possibly, modest truths, but truths all the same. It is for this reason that they are rare in any time and especially rare in our time, when whole industries exist for the sole purpose of cranking out lies. If Seamus Heaney has been granted the authority to write some living poems – the modest love poem to his wife entitled 'Poem', the heartfelt, awkward sonnets in memory of his mother – he should be able to overcome his uncertainty and rest assured they will survive when he is finally free of the gas-filled balloon of his contemporary reputation.

Selected Bibliography

Books by Seamus Heaney

Poetry

Death of a Naturalist (1966)
Door into the Dark (1969)
Wintering Out (1972)
North (1975)
Field Work (1979)
Poems 1965-1975 (1980)
Sweeney Astray (translation) (1983)
Station Island (1984)
The Haw Lantern (1987)
Selected Poems 1966-1987 (1990)
Seeing Things (1991)
The Spirit Level (1996)
Opened Ground: Poems 1966-1996 (1998)
Beowulf (translation) (1999)
Electric Light (2001)

Prose

Preoccupations: Selected Prose 1968-1978 (1980)
The Government of the Tongue (1988)
Crediting Poetry (The Nobel Lecture) (1996)

All of these books were published by Faber & Faber in London and by Farrar, Straus, and Giroux in New York.

Works on Seamus Heaney

Allen, Michael, ed. *Seamus Heaney: New Casebook Series* (London: MacMillan, 1997) This anthology of critical essays offers a wide range of views in one place.

Buttel, Robert, *Seamus Heaney* (Lewisburg, PA: Bucknell University Press, 1975)

Deane, Seamus, 'The Famous Seamus', *The New Yorker*, 20th March, 2000.

Hamilton, Ian, 'Excusez-Moi', *London Review of Books*, 1st October 1987.

Miller, Karl, interviewer. *Seamus Heaney in conversation with Karl Miller* (London: Between the Lines, 2000). This lengthy interview includes an extensive bibliography of criticism on Heaney.

Nye, Robert, 'Heaney Reaches a Blind Summit on Mount Parnassus', *The Scotsman*, 3rd October 1998.

Vendler, Helen, *Seamus Heaney* (Cambridge, MA: Harvard University Press, 1998).

GREENWICH EXCHANGE BOOKS

Greenwich Exchange Student Guides are critical studies of major or contemporary serious writers in English and selected European languages. The series is for the student, the teacher and 'common readers' and is an ideal resource for libraries. The *Times Educational Supplement* praised these books, saying, "The style of these guides has a pressure of meaning behind it. Students should learn from that ... If art is about selection, perception and taste, then this is it."

(ISBN prefix 1-871551- applies)
The series includes:
W.H. Auden by Stephen Wade (36-6)
Honoré de Balzac by Wendy Mercer (48-X)
William Blake by Peter Davies (27-7)
The Brontës by Peter Davies (24-2)
Robert Browning by John Lucas (59-5)
Samuel Taylor Coleridge by Andrew Keanie (64-1)
Joseph Conrad by Martin Seymour-Smith (18-8)
William Cowper by Michael Thorn (25-0)
Charles Dickens by Robert Giddings (26-9)
Emily Dickinson by Marnie Pomeroy (68-4)
John Donne by Sean Haldane (23-4)
Ford Madox Ford by Anthony Fowles (63-3)
The Stagecraft of Brian Friel by David Grant (74-9)
Robert Frost by Warren Hope (70-6)
Thomas Hardy by Sean Haldane (33-1)
Seamus Heaney by Warren Hope (37-4)
James Joyce by Michael Murphy (73-0)
Philip Larkin by Warren Hope (35-8)
Laughter in the Dark – The Plays of Joe Orton by Arthur Burke (56-0)
Philip Roth by Paul McDonald (72-2)
Shakespeare's *Macbeth* by Matt Simpson (69-2)
Shakespeare's *Othello* by Matt Simpson (71-4)
Shakespeare's *The Tempest* by Matt Simpson (75-7)
Shakespeare's Non-Dramatic Poetry by Martin Seymour-Smith (22-6)
Shakespeare's Sonnets by Martin Seymour-Smith (38-2)
Tobias Smollett by Robert Giddings (21-8)
Alfred, Lord Tennyson by Michael Thorn (20-X)
William Wordsworth by Andrew Keanie (57-9)

OTHER GREENWICH EXCHANGE BOOKS

Paperback unless otherwise stated.

Shakespeare's Sonnets
Martin Seymour-Smith
Martin Seymour-Smith's outstanding achievement lies in the field of literary biography and criticism. In 1963 he produced his comprehensive edition, in the old spelling, of *Shakespeare's Sonnets* (here revised and corrected by himself and Peter Davies in 1998). With its landmark introduction and its brilliant critical commentary on each sonnet, it was praised by William Empson and John Dover Wilson. Stephen Spender said of him "I greatly admire Martin Seymour-Smith for the independence of his views and the great interest of his mind"; and both Robert Graves and Anthony Burgess described him as the leading critic of his time. His exegesis of the *Sonnets* remains unsurpassed.
2001 • 194 pages • ISBN 1-871551-38-2

English Language Skills
Vera Hughes
If you want to be sure, (as a student, or in your business or personal life), that your written English is correct, this book is for you. Vera Hughes' aim is to help you remember the basic rules of spelling, grammar and punctuation. 'Noun', 'verb', 'subject', 'object' and 'adjective' are the only technical terms used. The book teaches the clear, accurate English required by the business and office world. It coaches acceptable current usage and makes the rules easier to remember.
Vera Hughes was a civil servant and is a trainer and author of training manuals.
2002 • 142 pages • ISBN 1-871551-60-9

LITERARY CRITICISM

The Author, the Book and the Reader
Robert Giddings
This collection of essays analyses the effects of changing technology and the attendant commercial pressures on literary styles and subject matter. Authors covered include Charles Dickens, Tobias George Smollett, Mark Twain, Dr Johnson and John le Carré.
1991 • 220 pages • illustrated • ISBN 1-871551-01-3

John Dryden
Anthony Fowles

Of all the poets of the Augustan age, John Dryden was the most worldly. Anthony Fowles traces Dryden's evolution from 'wordsmith' to major poet. This critical study shows a poet of vigour and technical panache whose art was forged in the heat and battle of a turbulent polemical and pamphleteering age. Although Dryden's status as a literary critic has long been established, Fowles draws attention to Dryden's neglected achievements as a translator of poetry. He deals also with the less well-known aspects of Dryden's work – his plays and occasional pieces.

Born in London and educated at the Universities of Oxford and Southern California, Anthony Fowles began his career in filmmaking before becoming an author of film and television scripts and more than twenty books. Readers will welcome the many contemporary references to novels and film with which Fowles illuminates the life and work of this decisively influential English poetic voice.

2003 • 292 pages • ISBN 1-871551-58-7

Liar! Liar!: Jack Kerouac – Novelist
R.J. Ellis

The fullest study of Jack Kerouac's fiction to date. It is the first book to devote an individual chapter to every one of his novels. *On the Road, Visions of Cody* and *The Subterraneans* are reread in-depth, in a new and exciting way. *Visions of Gerard* and *Doctor Sax* are also strikingly reinterpreted, as are other daringly innovative writings, like 'The Railroad Earth' and his "try at a spontaneous *Finnegans Wake*" – *Old Angel Midnight*. Neglected writings, such as *Tristessa* and *Big Sur*, are also analysed, alongside better-known novels such as *Dharma Bums* and *Desolation Angels*.

R.J. Ellis is Senior Lecturer in English at Nottingham Trent University.

1999 • 295 pages • ISBN 1-871551-53-6

BIOGRAPHY

The Good That We Do
John Lucas

John Lucas' book blends fiction, biography and social history in order to tell the story of his grandfather, Horace Kelly. Headteacher of a succession of elementary schools in impoverished areas of London, 'Hod' Kelly was also a keen cricketer, a devotee of the music hall, and included among his friends the great Trade Union leader, Ernest Bevin. In telling the story of his life, Lucas has provided a fascinating range of insights into the lives of ordinary Londoners from the First World War until the outbreak of the

Second World War. Threaded throughout is an account of such people's hunger for education, and of the different ways government, church and educational officialdom ministered to that hunger. *The Good That We Do* is both a study of one man and of a period when England changed, drastically and forever.

John Lucas is Professor of English at Nottingham Trent University and is a poet and critic.

2001 • 214 pages • ISBN 1-871551-54-4

In Pursuit of Lewis Carroll

Raphael Shaberman

Sherlock Holmes and the author uncover new evidence in their investigations into the mysterious life and writing of Lewis Carroll. They examine published works by Carroll that have been overlooked by previous commentators. A newly discovered poem, almost certainly by Carroll, is published here.

Amongst many aspects of Carroll's highly complex personality, this book explores his relationship with his parents, numerous child friends, and the formidable Mrs Liddell, mother of the immortal Alice. Raphael Shaberman was a founder member of the Lewis Carroll Society and a teacher of autistic children.

1994 • 118 pages • illustrated • ISBN 1-871551-13-7

Musical Offering

Yolanthe Leigh

In a series of vivid sketches, anecdotes and reflections, Yolanthe Leigh tells the story of her growing up in the Poland of the 1930s and the Second World War. These are poignant episodes of a child's first encounters with both the enchantments and the cruelties of the world; and from a later time, stark memories of the brutality of the Nazi invasion, and the hardships of student life in Warsaw under the Occupation. But most of all this is a record of inward development; passages of remarkable intensity and simplicity describe the girl's response to religion, to music, and to her discovery of philosophy.

Yolanthe Leigh was formerly a Lecturer in Philosophy at Reading University.

2000 • 57 pages • ISBN: 1-871551-46-3

Norman Cameron

Warren Hope

Norman Cameron's poetry was admired by W.H. Auden, celebrated by Dylan Thomas and valued by Robert Graves. He was described by Martin Seymour-Smith as, "one of ... the most rewarding and pure poets of his generation ..." and is at last given a full length biography. This eminently sociable man, who had periods of darkness and despair, wrote little poetry by comparison with others of his time, but always of a consistently high quality – imaginative and profound.

2000 • 221 pages • illustrated • ISBN 1-871551-05-6

POETRY

Adam's Thoughts in Winter
Warren Hope

Warren Hope's poems have appeared from time to time in a number of literary periodicals, pamphlets and anthologies on both sides of the Atlantic. They appeal to lovers of poetry everywhere. His poems are brief, clear, frequently lyrical, characterised by wit, but often distinguished by tenderness. The poems gathered in this first book-length collection counter the brutalising ethos of contemporary life, speaking of and for the virtues of modesty, honesty and gentleness in an individual, memorable way.

2000 • 47 pages • ISBN 1-871551-40-4

Baudelaire: Les Fleurs du Mal
Translated by F.W. Leakey

Selected poems from *Les Fleurs du Mal* are translated with parallel French texts and are designed to be read with pleasure by readers who have no French as well as those who are practised in the French language.

F.W. Leakey was Professor of French in the University of London. As a scholar, critic and teacher he specialised in the work of Baudelaire for 50 years and published a number of books on the poet.

2001 • 153 pages • ISBN 1-871551-10-2

Lines from the Stone Age
Sean Haldane

Reviewing Sean Haldane's 1992 volume *Desire in Belfast*, Robert Nye wrote in *The Times* that "Haldane can be sure of his place among the English poets." This place is not yet a conspicuous one, mainly because his early volumes appeared in Canada and because he has earned his living by other means than literature. Despite this, his poems have always had their circle of readers. The 60 previously unpublished poems of *Lines from the Stone Age* – "lines of longing, terror, pride, lust and pain" – may widen this circle.

2000 • 53 pages • ISBN 1-871551-39-0

Wilderness
Martin Seymour-Smith

This is Martin Seymour-Smith's first publication of his poetry for more than twenty years. This collection of 36 poems is a fearless account of an inner life of love, frustration, guilt, laughter and the celebration of others. He is best known to the general public as the author of the controversial and bestselling *Hardy* (1994).

1994 • 52 pages • ISBN 1-871551-08-0